Forming the Assembly
TO CELEBRATE
THE MASS

Forming the Assembly
TO CELEBRATE
THE MASS

Lawrence E. Mick

LITURGY
TRAINING
PUBLICATIONS

Forming the Assembly to Celebrate the Mass
© 2002 Archdiocese of Chicago: Liturgy Training
Publications, 1800 North Hermitage Avenue,
Chicago IL 60622-1101; 1-800-933-1800; fax
1-800-933-7094; orders@ltp.org; www.ltp.org.
All rights reserved.

Visit our website at www.ltp.org.

This book was edited by Lorie Simmons with
assistance from Vicky Tufano and Laura Goodman.
Audrey Novak Riley was the production editor. The
design is by Lucy Smith, and the typesetting was
done by Anne Fritzinger in Minion. Cover photo
© Bill Wittman. Cover and interior art by Suzanne
Novak. Printed by Sentinel Printing Company, Inc.,
in St. Cloud, Minnesota.

Library of Congress Control Number: 2002109383

ISBN 1-56854-430-8

FAMAS

Introduction

LITURGICAL FORMATION FOR YOUR PARISH

Celebrating liturgy well doesn't come naturally. The symbols, prayers and ritual actions of the liturgy must be learned and understood in order to celebrate and enter into the meaning of the liturgy. Liturgical formation of the people of God is an ongoing need in every parish. Although this need has become more obvious since the Second Vatican Council set us on the course of liturgical reform, catechesis for worship is needed in every age. The faithful have both a right and a duty to take part in the liturgy with understanding and competence. This is one of the fundamental insights and goals of the liturgical movement.

THE LITURGICAL MOVEMENT

The modern liturgical movement has a long history, extending back at least into the nineteenth century. Throughout that time liturgists in various centers in Germany, France and Belgium were conducting research into the history of the liturgy and making pastoral adaptations of the liturgy.

The movement grew from a concern that people had become disconnected from the liturgy at a time when the emerging modern world needed to be nourished by the deep mysteries of the faith. Theologians and liturgists felt a pastoral desire to help people benefit more from the riches of the liturgy. Historical insights about how the early Christians had worshiped in an age of great vitality in the church led to efforts to seek a similar vitality in the modern age.

In the 1920s, the liturgical movement took root in the United States, though it remained the concern of relatively few Catholics until the Second Vatican Council. Pioneers in the liturgical movement in the United States saw the renewal of the liturgy as the key to the renewal of the faithful. Such a renewed church could then be more effective in renewing society and dealing with social problems in light of the gospel.

The Second Vatican Council met from 1962 to 1965, and it also saw the renewal of the liturgy as the key to renewing the church. The first document the Council issued was the *Constitution on the Sacred Liturgy,* dated December 4, 1963.

With the publication of this constitution, the liturgical renewal gained the attention of the whole church. Though various aspects of liturgical reform had been adopted and taught by several popes through the first half of the twentieth century, the broad scope of the reforms mandated by the Second Vatican Council ensured that every Catholic would become aware of the revitalization of their liturgy.

In the decades since the promulgation of the *Constitution on the Sacred Liturgy,* major changes have been implemented in the worship life of parishes around the world. We have been revising liturgical books, learning a new liturgical repertoire of music and texts and actions, developing new liturgical ministries and adapting to new liturgical rituals.

WHAT'S OUR NEXT STEP IN THE LITURGICAL MOVEMENT?

Every movement and every reform has its stages. Some think this first stage, now somewhat complete, marks the end of the liturgical reform. Such a view is seriously mistaken, however. History teaches us that the church's liturgy is always in some degree of flux and development. Like the church itself, which Vatican II called *"semper reformanda"* (always in need of reform), the liturgy is always in need of further development.

At this stage in the process, however, it seems opportune to consider a deeper need. While scholars and composers and committees continue the work of refining liturgical books and providing new resources, the more pressing need on the pastoral level seems to be a deeper liturgical formation of the people of God. Members of the assembly need and deserve to understand the liturgy more fully so that they can benefit from the spiritual riches that the liturgy offers.

USING THIS BOOK

This little book is designed to assist that effort, and it speaks to several audiences. It addresses parish leaders—those who have the responsibility of preparing the celebrations of the liturgy and of forming liturgical ministers and members of the assembly. It will also be useful in adult and youth catechesis and to any individuals who wish to deepen their appreciation of worship in order to drink more deeply from the source and summit of the church's activity.

Questions to foster reflection and discussion will be found at the end of each chapter. Solo readers are encouraged to take time to reflect and pray over these questions in order to make the ideas addressed in each chapter a source of personal spiritual growth. Discussion groups or parish committees might use the same questions to spark conversation that can lead to further insights and perhaps to some improvements in the way the liturgy is celebrated in the local community of faith. Space has been provided after each question for the reader's notes.

The substance of this work appeared first as a series of articles in *Today's Parish* magazine. The author wishes to acknowledge the support and encouragement offered by the editor of that publication, Daniel Connors.

Chapter 1

The Challenge of Renewal

THE LITURGICAL MOVEMENT: EARLY DEVELOPMENTS

It will soon be a half-century since the publication of the *Constitution on the Sacred Liturgy,* issued by the Second Vatican Council on December 4, 1963. After decades on this journey of liturgical reform, one might well ask if we are any closer to the promised land foreseen by the Council.

To gain perspective on how far we have come, let's look back to the beginning of the twentieth century. Often people assume that the liturgical renewal began with the Second Vatican Council (1962–1965), but it really began long before Pope John XXIII even dreamed of the Council.

Much research and pastoral work done in the nineteenth century provided the basis for the liturgical movement in the twentieth century. Studies of Christian initiation as it was practiced in the third, fourth and fifth centuries, for example, led to the restoration of the catechumenate in the twentieth century. The text of the second eucharistic prayer in our Mass today was inspired by a prayer found in a third-century document called the *Apostolic Tradition*. Perhaps the most important insight from history was the active role of the faithful in the celebration of the liturgy in the early church.

This work began to receive official approval under Pope Saint Pius X at the beginning of the twentieth century. His 1903 *Motu Proprio* on sacred music called for the active participation of the people in the liturgy. He lowered the age for first communion in 1910 and encouraged frequent communion. He also authorized reforms in both the calendar and the Liturgy of the Hours during his pontificate. Pope Pius XI, in his encyclical *Divini Cultus* in 1928, reaffirmed the teachings of Pius X.

Pope Pius XII issued two encyclicals that are significant for the liturgical movement. In 1943, *Mystici Corporis (The Mystical Body)* revived the ancient image of the church as the body of Christ and presented the liturgy as a work of that body which unifies the members in the power of the Spirit.

Four years later, Pius XII issued an encyclical on the liturgy itself, titled *Mediator Dei*. Ideas and language from this encyclical found their way into the *Constitution on the Sacred Liturgy* promulgated by the Second Vatican Council. Pius XII spoke of Christ's presence in the priest who presides, in the eucharistic species and in the assembly who prays to God. He insisted that the liturgy is offered by Christ and by the community gathered in him, by the whole body of Christ, head and members.

In the 1950s, Pius XII also issued revised rites for the Easter Vigil and then for the rest of Holy Week. These rites began the process of reforming the calendar and the liturgical seasons.

THE SECOND VATICAN COUNCIL

When Vatican II promulgated the *Constitution on the Sacred Liturgy*, therefore, it was continuing a movement that had been underway throughout the century. The Council ratified the liturgical movement and called for a thorough reform and renewal of the whole of the church's liturgical life.

The widespread attention given to the Council and the changes it mandated brought liturgical reform to the attention of most Catholics. The Council was too newsworthy to ignore, whereas the encyclicals of Pius X, XI and XII had been read by few and rarely taught at the parish level. It was not until the 1950s and 1960s, for example, that most American Catholics began to receive communion weekly, though Pius X had called for this in 1910.

The lack of attention to the liturgical movement earlier in the twentieth century made it more difficult for many Catholics in this country to understand and embrace the changes mandated by the Council. Moreover, many of the church's leaders, including parish pastors, had little education in liturgical history or theology and were unprepared to help their communities adapt to the revised liturgy.

Such obstacles undoubtedly increased the level of resistance to the changes that many parishes have experienced. At the same time it must be noted that the vast majority of American Catholics have embraced the reformed liturgy with enthusiasm. Surveys consistently show that most Catholics are pleased with the major changes in our worship and have no desire to return to preconciliar forms of worship.

Parishes vary, of course, in the degree to which they have implemented the reform. Some have embraced both its letter and its spirit, while others have done only what was required by law (and a few even ignore that). Some parishes have offered their members a variety of opportunities to deepen their understanding of the liturgy and of the reasons behind the changes; others have offered very little.

Even in parishes that generally offer good liturgy, there is always room for improvement, but the reforms of the Second Vatican Council are now the basis of worship in most parishes. The new liturgical books are largely in place, the various ministries have been established and given training, musical programs have matured beyond the early days of vernacular liturgy, preaching has generally improved since the Council and many people now take an active part in the celebration of the liturgy.

THE GOALS OF THE REFORM

We can truly rejoice in the progress that we have made over the past decades. There is, however, no room for complacency. The goals of the Second Vatican Council went beyond reforming rituals and issuing new books. Let's look more closely at these goals.

The *Constitution on the Sacred Liturgy* was the first major document issued by the Council; it begins by stating the purposes of the Council itself:

> This Sacred Council has several aims in view: it desires to impart an ever increasing vigor to the Christian life of the faithful; to adapt more suitably to the needs of our own times those institutions that are subject to change; to foster whatever can promote union among all who believe in Christ; to strengthen whatever can help to call the whole of humanity into the household of the Church. The Council therefore sees particularly cogent reasons for undertaking the reform and promotion of the liturgy. (CSL, 1, in *The*

Liturgy Documents: A Parish Resource, vol. 1, 3rd ed.
[Chicago: Liturgy Training Publications, 1991]; subsequent
citations are to this edition.)

The document continues by speaking specifically about the role
of liturgy in accomplishing these aims:

> For the liturgy, "making the work of our redemption a
> present actuality," most of all in the divine sacrifice of the
> eucharist, is the outstanding means whereby the faithful
> may express in their lives and manifest to others the
> mystery of Christ and the real nature of the true Church.
> It is of the essence of the Church to be both human and
> divine, visible yet endowed with invisible resources, eager
> to act yet intent on contemplation, present in this world yet
> not at home in it; and the Church is all these things in such
> wise that in it the human is directed and subordinated to
> the divine, the visible likewise to the invisible, action
> to contemplation, and this present world to that city yet
> to come which we seek. While the liturgy daily builds up
> those who are within into a holy temple of the Lord, into a
> dwelling place for God in the Spirit, to the mature measure
> of the fullness of Christ, at the same time it marvelously
> strengthens their power to preach Christ and thus shows
> forth the Church to those who are outside as a sign lifted up
> among the nations, under which the scattered children of
> God may be gathered together, until there is one sheepfold
> and one shepherd. (CSL, 2)

It is important to note that the Council saw the reform and promotion of the liturgy as a primary means of achieving the goals of the Council as a whole. Its overarching purpose was to renew the life of the church.

Thus the goal of the liturgical reforms was not to create new rituals or publish new books, but to create new hearts and a new spirit among the Christian faithful. Ultimately, we can only judge the success of the liturgical reforms by evaluating their effect on the renewal of Christian life among the members of the church.

While it is important to continue improving the celebration of the liturgy itself, perhaps it is also time to tackle more explicitly the deeper goal of the reforms—the renewal of the Christian faithful. What this requires, first of all, is a deeper understanding of the liturgy and a deeper involvement in the liturgical action.

How the Liturgy Works

The twin purposes of the liturgy can be simply stated: to praise God and to transform the worshipers. In one sense it is a single purpose, for God is praised when we are transformed into the image of Christ.

The liturgy accomplishes our transformation both gradually and subtly—primarily through the power of symbolic action. The symbols of the liturgy invite us into a different experience than our usual activities. They allow us to experience the kingdom of God and to commit ourselves to work for the coming of that kingdom.

For any fruitful transformation to occur, however, the cooperation of the worshiper is necessary. Our tradition insists that the sacraments are valid even if the minister is unworthy, a teaching expressed by the Latin phrase *ex opere operato*. The spiritual fruitfulness of that sacrament, however, depends also on the response of those who participate in it, a truth expressed in the companion phrase *ex opere operantis.*

The challenge facing us then is to find effective ways to help parishioners enter fully into the liturgy. This requires both understanding and openness on the part of each worshiper. Members of the assembly need to become aware of the meaning of the worship and then choose to embrace that meaning in their own lives.

Surrendering Ourselves to the Liturgy

A first step for many people is to realize that we must surrender ourselves to the liturgy—that is, allow ourselves to be formed by it. In the spiritual life, a key strategy for opening oneself to the Spirit is letting go of self, giving in to God's will for us. Surrendering ourselves to the liturgy is similar. Liturgical celebration offers us many benefits, but it also makes significant demands upon us. Our experience is most fruitful when we enter fully into the dynamics of the liturgy.

Liturgy is not simply a human creation. It relies on human words and actions and meanings, but the liturgy has been given to us by the Lord through the tradition of the church, and we can shape it only within certain parameters. If the liturgy is to be a means for us to encounter the divine presence, we must do so on God's terms, not ours.

Thus entering into the liturgy requires a certain openness from us. It requires letting go of our preferences and desires. Often we must also surrender our expectations and seek rather to fulfill God's expectations of us.

Surrender is never easy. It may be especially difficult in our society, which tends to see surrender as an act of weakness and places so much emphasis on individual achievements. In fact, surrender requires great strength of spirit, and it may be the hardest thing each of us must do. Surrender to God is the basic dynamic of the spiritual life.

JOINING A COMMUNAL ACTION

That surrender often finds its first expression in our willingness to enter into one communal act of worship. This is not easy for members of an individualistic society like our own. We frequently come to church focused on ourselves, our needs, our problems, our concerns. It takes a conscious decision to put most of that aside and enter into a joint act of worship that we all share with Christ himself.

This may be doubly difficult for Catholics whose understanding of liturgy was formed before Vatican II. Worship then was rather individualistic. Parishioners came to church on Sunday and were free to pray as each one chose. Some followed the priest with an English-Latin missal. Others said the rosary. Some prayed novenas. Others had their own series of prayers. Worshipers were present at the Mass, but were not necessarily praying the Mass.

Conditioned by a history of such individualistic worship and living in an individualistic culture, many find it hard to learn how to enter into one common act of worship. The prayer and sacrifice we offer are that of Christ himself. Each of us is called to join with Christ in offering praise and thanksgiving to the Father.

Pope John Paul II spoke of the communal nature of both our worship and our salvation in his 1998 apostolic letter *Dies Domini:*

> Those who have received the grace of baptism are not saved
> as individuals alone, but as members of the mystical body,
> having become part of the People of God. It is important
> therefore that they come together to express fully the very
> identity of the church, the *ekklesia,* the assembly called

together by the Risen Lord who offered his life "to reunite the scattered children of God" (John 11:52). They have become one in Christ (cf. Galatians 3:28) through the gift of the Spirit. This unity becomes visible when Christians gather together: It is then that they come to know vividly and to testify to the world that they are the people redeemed, drawn "from every tribe and language and people and nation" (Revelation 5:9). (DD, 31, in *The Liturgy Documents: A Parish Resource,* vol. 2 [Chicago: Liturgy Training Publications, 1999]; subsequent citations are to this edition.)

Later in the same letter, the Holy Father speaks of the Day of the Lord as also the Day of the Church:

Therefore, the *dies Domini* is also the *dies Ecclesiae.* This is why on the pastoral level the community aspect of the Sunday celebration should be particularly stressed. As I have noted elsewhere, among the many activities of a parish, "none is as vital or as community-forming as the Sunday celebration of the Lord's Day and his eucharist." Mindful of this, the Second Vatican Council recalled that efforts must be made to ensure that there is "within the parish, a lively sense of community, in the first place through the community celebration of Sunday Mass." (#35)

Many Catholics today still need to understand and embrace this essential community aspect of our worship. Continual catechesis on this topic will be needed to counteract the individualistic tendencies of our culture.

Sharing Christ's Sacrifice

Joining in one common act of worship is essential to the proper understanding of the Mass as a sacrifice. Whereas in the Old Testament many varieties of plant and animal sacrifice were practiced, there is only one acceptable sacrifice in the New Testament— that of Christ himself. The Mass is a sacrifice because it brings us into contact with that eternal sacrifice of Christ. We share in it by joining ourselves to Christ's act of worship of the Father.

The profound meanings tied to our sharing in this sacrificial act of worship bring us to the heart of Christianity and the heart of the eucharist. The death and resurrection of the Lord Jesus is the central fact of history and the central theme of Christian spirituality. Helping parishioners to share Christ's act of worship with one another is a basic goal of liturgical formation.

Transformed into Transformers

Only by entering fully into the movement of the liturgy itself do we allow God to transform us into the image of God's Son. If we hold ourselves back, we hinder the action of God's grace within us. If we try to maintain our separation from our brothers and sisters, we resist God's efforts to form us into the one body of Christ.

If we enter fully into the action of the liturgy, then God can shape our minds and our hearts according to the divine will. Then we will become effective instruments of God's will in our world. Empowered by God's grace, we who have been transformed can be used by God to transform our world.

That is the ultimate goal of the liturgical renewal—to transform the world for Christ. Liturgy leads to mission, and those who share in Christ's sacrificial worship are led to share in his sacrificial life and love.

Just the Beginning

There are those who claim that the liturgical renewal is over, and there are even some who seem determined to reverse the progress of recent decades. Far from being over, the liturgical renewal is still in its infancy. It is time to begin feeding the people of God the rich fare that the liturgy offers them. This is the primary pastoral task that must be embraced by all parish ministers. Liturgy is not just for liturgists. It is the source and summit of our life together in Christ. It should be the center of all our efforts to renew the church as the Second Vatican Council desired.

Questions for Reflection and Discussion

1. What new information or perspectives did you gain from the teachings of the popes who called for liturgical reform prior to Vatican II? How could you share these with members of your parish?

2. If you remember the beginning of the changes in the liturgy following the Second Vatican Council, try to recall your first reactions. How much catechesis about the changes do you remember? Did you welcome or resist the changes? Why? If you do not remember it yourself, what do you remember hearing from others about the changes? about the time before the changes?

3. The Council saw the renewal of the liturgy as key to accomplishing the goals of the Council itself. In what ways do you see the liturgy furthering those goals? In what ways has the liturgy

not furthered the Council's goals? (You may refer to your experiences at other parishes as well as to those at your current parish.) What is needed to move this process forward today?

4. In what ways have the reforms of the liturgy led to a real renewal of the church? What evidence do you see of such renewal? What areas do you think have been missed?

5. Do you find it hard to surrender yourself to the liturgy? Why or why not? Do you think others in your parish have difficulty doing this? How can we help people to understand the importance of such self-surrender?

6. How would you explain the difference between praying individually during the liturgy and joining in one communal act of worship? Why do you think some people find it difficult to enter into such communal prayer? How can we help them learn to do so?

7. The liturgy is meant to transform us. On what occasions do you remember being changed by your participation in the church's worship? What signs of transformation do you see in your community of faith? If you see none, why might this be?

Chapter 2

Entering into the Liturgy

A lthough the introductory rites mark the formal beginning of the Mass, the process of entering into the dynamics of the liturgy begins earlier than the opening song. The *General Instruction of the Roman Missal* states the purpose of the introductory rites: "that the faithful coming together take on the form of a community and prepare themselves to listen properly to God's word and celebrate the Eucharist worthily" (IGRM, 46, from Secretariat for the Liturgy, "An English Language Study Translation" [Washington: National Conference of Catholic Bishops, 2000]). Realistically speaking, unless the participants are predisposed to being formed and prepared as a community, no set of minor rituals can really accomplish that goal. But the rituals with which we begin a celebration can remind people that they are a community of faith and help them focus their attention on the word to be proclaimed and the sacrificial meal to be celebrated. To be effective, participants must approach the introductory rites with a receptive attitude and an understanding of the liturgy that they begin.

THE PRESENCE OF CHRIST

The most important area of understanding (and misunderstanding) concerns the presence of Christ in the liturgy. Many Catholics still link the presence of Christ primarily with the presence of the reserved sacrament in the tabernacle. This has led to terrible arguments and accusations when parishes build or renovate their worship spaces and create a separate chapel of reservation for the reserved sacrament, as many Vatican documents have urged. The vehemence with which these arguments are conducted indicates how completely some people's awareness of Christ's presence is linked solely to the reserved sacrament.

Our tradition teaches otherwise, however. That tradition speaks of at least four ways that Christ is present in the eucharist: in the assembly gathered, in the priest presiding, in the word proclaimed and in the meal shared. The presence of Christ in the tabernacle is derivative of and secondary to his living presence in the celebration of the eucharist itself.

Much more preaching and catechetical effort must be devoted to helping people recognize Christ in all the ways that he is present in the eucharist. And the mode of his presence that needs the most attention is his presence in the assembly itself. As we noted in the previous chapter, this is not a new teaching. It comes from the long tradition of the church and was reemphasized before Vatican II in the teachings of Pope Pius XII.

In his 1947 encyclical on the liturgy, *Mediator Dei,* Pope Pius XII wrote about the ways that Christ is present in the liturgy:

Along with the Church, therefore, her Divine Founder is present at every liturgical function: Christ is present at the august sacrifice of the altar both in the person of His minister and above all under the eucharistic species. He is present in the sacraments, infusing into them the power which makes them ready instruments of sanctification. He is present, finally, in prayer of praise and petition we direct to God, as it is written: "Where there are two or three gathered together in My Name, there am I in the midst of them." The sacred liturgy is, consequently, the public worship which our Redeemer as Head of the Church renders to the Father, as well as the worship which the community of the faithful renders to its Founder, and through Him to the heavenly Father. It is, in short, the worship rendered by the Mystical Body of Christ in the entirety of its Head and members. (#20, http://www. vatican.va/holy_father/pius_xii/encyclicals/documents/ hf_p-xii_enc_20111947_mediator-dei_en.html [accessed July 2, 2002])

Though he does not explicitly mention Christ's presence in the word, the pope makes clear Christ's presence in the priest, in the eucharistic species and wherever two or three are gathered in his name.

THE BODY OF CHRIST AT WORSHIP

The pontiff also notes that the liturgy is the worship rendered by the mystical body of Christ in the entirety of its head and members. Remembering and affirming their identity as the body of Christ is a primary task of those who assemble for worship. This means both recognizing one another as members of one body and recognizing the presence of Christ who is the head of that body.

At this point it is essential to take the "both-and" view rather than the "either-or" view. Too often the issue is seen as either recognizing God's presence or recognizing one another. Both are indispensable and ultimately inseparable. It is not adequate to focus only on the presence of Christ in isolation from the members of his body, nor is it sufficient to focus only on the members without recognizing the presence of Christ.

Proper liturgical hospitality goes beyond sociability and friendliness; community at the liturgy is different from social or political unity. Both depend on a vital awareness of the presence of the Lord. It is Christ's presence that forms us into one body, the community of faith. It is Christ's presence that we welcome when we extend hospitable concern to those who gather to worship with us.

This flows from the fundamental principle of Christianity, namely, incarnation. The incarnation is not only the historical event of the Son of God becoming human two millennia ago. It continues in the church, which is now the body of Christ. To deny the presence of Christ in the church assembled is certainly untraditional, if not actually heretical. Yet many Catholics do not understand this part of our tradition and deny the truth of it, in theory or in practice. They deserve to be taught this marvelous mystery of Christ's presence among us, or they will never fully appreciate the richness of the liturgy.

Though some of this teaching can be explained verbally, much of it will be communicated most effectively in practice. People need to be encouraged to greet one another in Christ before the liturgy, to reconnect with other parts of the body of Christ, to express the loving concern for one another that binds us in Christ. Hospitality at

Mass must not be mistaken for idle chit-chat before the liturgy. It recognizes Christ in one another and shares the love of Christ with each other.

Experience has taught us that a good gathering space outside the actual worship space is very helpful in fostering a more hospitable assembly. Even there, however, it is important to call people to a deeper sense of unity than mere sociability. If you are not blessed with such a gathering space, then the assembly needs to learn to express hospitality in the worship space itself. This can be a challenge if the tabernacle is in the worship space, since some people feel irreverent engaging each other in its vicinity. But the caring, respectful sort of greeting described here would not be inappropriate.

BEING PART OF THE BODY

The issue of hospitality is basically a question of our willingness to be a part of the body of Christ. Especially in the United States, we are very conscious of our individuality and very protective of our privacy. To open ourselves to others is always a risk; it makes us vulnerable. Worshiping together as one body in Christ requires a conscious decision to take that risk, to go out of ourselves in order to join with others in a common act of worship.

This act of surrender is the first step in entering into the sacrifice of Christ. Christ, too, had to take the risk of becoming vulnerable in order to do the Father's will. He surrendered himself for the sake of his brothers and sisters, and we are called to follow his example. Some people find this first step more difficult than others do, but all of us must overcome the instinct to defensiveness that inclines us to maintain our separation and distance.

It is important that worshipers understand the necessity of making this effort. They need to know that this is not just a matter of protocol or the desire of the pastor to have lively worship. The issue is whether or not they truly enter into the dynamics of the liturgy, which in turn determines how much they will benefit from it. The goal of the eucharistic liturgy is to transform us more fully into the body of Christ. This is only possible if we are willing to be part of the body.

SITTING TOGETHER

In many parishes a good indicator of whether worshipers are willing to be one body is the way they seat themselves. If we are to be the body of Christ at worship, then we must sit together as much as possible. Sitting in close proximity enables us to sing together and to pray together with one voice because we are able to hear one another.

Conversely, a worshiping assembly that refuses to sit together is really refusing to be an assembly, refusing to join together as one body. Liturgy is not merely internal intention. That intention must be expressed by external action. We don't want empty ritual that means nothing, but what we mean must be expressed by our actions.

Of course, it does not work well to try to force people to sit together. More effective would be a long-term effort to help people understand the importance of being close together in order to worship well together.

THE OPENING SONG

The Roman rite does not really call for a closing song at the end of Mass (though it does not forbid it, either), but it clearly calls for an opening song. This suggests that the opening song has an important function in the liturgy.

Once people have gathered together physically and welcomed Christ in their midst by welcoming one another, the entrance song enables them to join their voices into one voice. This is one of the key functions of communal song—it enables us to speak together in a way that is intelligible because the rhythm of the music keeps us together. For contrast, listen sometime to how unclear the recitation of the creed can become as people proceed at slightly different rates.

Another function of the opening song is to proclaim the focus of the celebration or the season of the liturgical year. It "sets the theme" for the rest of the liturgy, and the involvement of all present in this opening act of praise sets the pattern for full involvement in the whole celebration.

And how can this full involvement be fostered? Instead of just urging everyone to sing, choose an opening song that everyone knows and can sing easily. This is not the place to introduce a new song unless it has been thoroughly taught for several weeks in advance. An opening song that people do not know or cannot sing easily can discourage participation in the rest of the liturgy.

INTRODUCTORY RITES

After the opening song, the liturgy includes a variety of elements in the introductory rites. The greeting at the beginning of the liturgy is drawn from the scriptures, so it should not be replaced by more casual language. Though "Good morning" may seem friendly, Christians can greet one another with more significant words, especially in a formal setting like worship.

The penitential rite often poses a problem, for its role in the eucharistic liturgy is easily misunderstood. If the emphasis is placed on recalling our sins and feeling guilty, many people conclude that this is a quick substitute for the sacrament of penance. The proper function of this brief ritual, however, is to remind us of the mercy of God—another reason to celebrate and to give thanks. This understanding of the rite calls for some catechesis, but it can also be furthered by the choice of texts. Consider, for example, the difference between saying "Let us call to mind our sins" and saying "Let us call to mind God's mercy."

The penitential rite is sometimes replaced by the sprinkling rite, which is especially appropriate during the Easter season. Though the baptismal significance of this ritual is fairly obvious, it can be highlighted by singing an acclamation that refers to baptism as the sprinkling is done.

The Glory to God is sung on most Sundays and major feasts. It seems best to sing rather than recite this text whenever it is used; simple musical settings for times outside the major festal seasons would be most appropriate. It might help the assembly to enter into this exalted moment of praise if the presider invites them by saying "Let us now lift our voices together in praise of our loving God" or something similar.

The most important element of the introductory rites is the opening prayer. It is also apparently the oldest element of these rituals. The only thing that may be older is the silent prayer that precedes it. (Remember how we begin on Good Friday with silent prostration.) Unfortunately the silence is often omitted or is so brief that it is ineffective. After the presider says, "Let us pray," there is supposed to be time for people to do just that. Only after a period of silent prayer does the presider sum it up in the collect prayer.

For people to enter into this moment of prayer, however, catechesis about the reason for the pause might be needed. It might be wise to start with a shorter pause (fifteen seconds?) and then gradually lengthen it as people become more comfortable with the silence. As a goal, consider increasing it until you reach a full minute. This can be a powerful reminder to the assembled worshipers that they are called to pray the liturgy, not just to attend it.

START THE RITE RIGHT

If the liturgy is to have the best effect—transforming people to love and serve—we have to set an appropriate tone at the beginning. Though the introductory rites are minor rites, not comparing in importance to the liturgy of the word or the liturgy of the eucharist, they are still crucial in inviting people into the action of the liturgy. Time spent doing these rituals well and instructing the people on their meaning and spiritual significance will be time well spent in any parish.

QUESTIONS FOR REFLECTION AND DISCUSSION

1. How would you explain the importance of the introductory rites of the Mass? In your parish, are they achieving their stated purpose to form us into a community and prepare us to hear the word of God? What could make them more effective?

2. Do you think most members of your Sunday assembly are aware of the presence of Christ in one another? What signs of this awareness do you see? How could it be heightened?

3. What gestures of hospitality would a visitor experience in your worshiping assembly? What could be done to improve the atmosphere of hospitality at worship? How do we keep such efforts from being reduced to mere sociability?

4. What evidence do you see that members of your assembly think of themselves as integral parts of the body of Christ? How can we help people recover a vital sense of this truth?

5. Describe the way people seat themselves for worship in your community: together in a group? scattered throughout the space? How does this arrangement affect the liturgy? If sitting together doesn't happen naturally, how can it be fostered?

6. How would you explain the importance of the opening song at the liturgy? Do your musicians regularly choose pieces that work well to fulfill the functions of the opening song?

7. How do the introductory rites in your worshiping community vary with the liturgical seasons? How does such variation affect your awareness of the season?

8. What parts of the introductory rites do you think are the most important? Is this reflected in the way they are carried out and the time given to them? What would make these rites more effective in your community?

Chapter 3

Standing under the Word

Years ago I remember seeing a poster that read: "To understand is to stand under, which is a good way to understand." This is especially true when we are speaking about the word of God. To understand it, we must stand under that word.

By standing under the word, I mean that we must place ourselves under the authority of the word if we are to understand it correctly. This word cannot be understood from a detached position. It is a word personally addressed to us by God, and it can only be properly understood in the context of that relationship. Because God is the one who is in charge of this relationship, we must come to accept God's will when it conflicts with our own. To understand the word, we must approach it with a willingness to be changed by it.

If one of the goals of the introductory rites is to prepare the assembly to hear the word of God, then the rites must lead the assembly to this attitude of openness and obedient listening. As we noted in the last chapter, the basic decision to enter into Christ's act of worship is part of an act of surrender that prepares the worshipers to stand under the word.

THE LITURGY OF THE WORD

A major obstacle to reaping the rich benefits of the liturgy of the word is a misunderstanding of the purpose of this part of the Mass. Many people think of this first half of the Mass as a time for education. They see it as an opportunity for Bible study, perhaps the Catholic version of Protestant Sunday school.

This approach leads people to see their role in the liturgy of the word as that of learners and their task as taking in all the ideas from the readings and the homily. This, of course, often leads to frustration because many of us are not familiar enough with the Bible to be able to fully comprehend the passages proclaimed during worship. People may feel that they need the text of the readings in hand so that they can follow along while the readings are proclaimed. Some even justify this by noting that you learn more if you involve more senses with the text.

Even those who are familiar with the scriptures may be frustrated if they assume that their task is to take it all in. Three readings, a psalm, an acclamation and a homily contain so many different ideas and themes that it would be a rare person who could really grasp all of it at one time.

The proper goal, it seems to me, is simply to hear the word of the Lord that God enables each of us to hear that day. Among all the words proclaimed and preached at a given celebration, there is surely a "word" (a sentence or a thought) that is meant for each of us, both personally and on behalf of the community. This word might console us or it might challenge us, but it will change us in some way if we hear it and embrace it.

In speaking of the liturgy of the word, Pope John Paul II notes in his apostolic letter, *Dies Domini:*

> It should also be borne in mind that the liturgical procla-
> mation of the word of God, especially in the Eucharistic
> assembly, is not so much a time for meditation and
> catechesis as a dialogue between God and his People, a
> dialogue in which the wonders of salvation are proclaimed
> and the demands of the Covenant are continually restated.
> On their part, the People of God are drawn to respond to
> this dialogue of love by giving thanks and praise, also by
> demonstrating their fidelity to the task of continual
> "conversion." (#41)

Worshipers need to recognize the role of the Holy Spirit in this dialogue. The Spirit inspired the scriptures when they were written. The Spirit enables the proclaimer to proclaim the word with power. The same Spirit, dwelling in each of us, enables us to hear the word of the Lord intended for us.

The 1982 *Introduction to the Lectionary for Mass* puts it this way:

> The working of the Holy Spirit precedes, accompanies, and
> brings to completion the whole celebration of the liturgy.
> But the Spirit also brings home to each person individually
> everything that in the proclamation of the word of God is
> spoken for the good of the whole assembly of the faithful.
> In strengthening the unity of all, the Holy Spirit at the same
> time fosters a diversity of gifts and furthers their multiform
> operation. (LMIn, 9, in *The Liturgy Documents: A Parish*

Resource, vol. 1, 3rd ed. [Chicago: Liturgy Training
Publications, 1991])

Any preacher who has stood at the church door after Mass has
probably had the experience of someone coming up and saying how
much he or she appreciated the homily, especially when the preacher
made a particular point—and it wasn't what the preacher said at
all! I think this is usually an indication that the Spirit enabled that
person to hear the word that he or she needed, whether or not it was
intended by the preacher. A preacher cannot preach 600 homilies to
touch each of 600 worshipers, but the Holy Spirit can.

We should be teaching the members of our parishes to be attentive to the Spirit and to listen for the word that God intends for
them to hear that day. It is far better to grasp one word or one idea
that God can use to change us than to try to get all the words and
leave Mass without any of them taking root.

The purpose of the liturgy of the word is not so much education as it is formation. We do not gather to learn about God; we
gather to meet God. We do not listen to learn about Christ; we listen
to Christ speaking to us today. Like the liturgy of the eucharist (the
table of the bread), the liturgy of the word (the table of the word) is
meant to nourish us with a spiritual experience of Christ's presence
for our sake.

RELINQUISHING CONTROL

One of the reasons we may have found it easier to approach the
liturgy of the word as education is that this allows us to feel in control of the process. To encounter the living Christ requires that we
give up control, and that is never easy for us.

One manifestation of this difficulty is the dependence of many assemblies on missals or other publications that contain the texts of the readings. While there are some people in every assembly who may need such aids, the ordinary response of worshipers to a proclaimed text should be to listen attentively, not to read along.

Experts on communication remind us that much of the communication process between people occurs beyond the words themselves. Body language, facial expressions, eye contact and other modes of communication are also involved, and most of those are lost if people are looking at their books rather than looking at the one speaking to them.

Books give us the feeling of being in control. With my own text I am not dependent on the reader. I can go at my own pace. I can reread a line several times; I can finish the reading before the lector. Having my own text puts me in charge of the word.

Yet the spiritual attitude necessary for fruitful reception of the word of God is one of humility, of standing under the word. We are not in control of the experience; God is. Rather than holding tightly to a book, we need to listen with open ears and hearts, ready to receive whatever the Lord chooses to give us. Open hands can be a symbol of that interior openness.

Listening is not a simple or a passive activity. It takes effort to focus our attention on the speaker and to ignore other internal or external distractions. This is the reverence that is required as our response to Christ's presence in the word. If Christ is truly speaking to us, then certainly we should be paying close attention to what he has to say. Such listening is itself a prayer, for prayer is not only talking to God but listening for what God has to tell us.

Preparing at Home

One of the things that hinders many people from fully benefiting from this part of the Mass is their unfamiliarity with the scriptures. All parishes should encourage scripture study, both individually and in groups. A solid introduction to the Bible with opportunities for ongoing study should be integral to all religious education curricula in the parish, for children and especially for adults.

Beyond this broader study of the Bible, it is important to teach parishioners the value of preparing for Sunday worship by reading the Sunday scriptures before coming to church. This can be fostered by listing the biblical citations in the bulletin the week before, but if the faithful are to adopt such preparation as their common practice, they will need steady encouragement from the pulpit and in bulletin notices.

Pope John Paul II encouraged such preparation in his apostolic letter, *Dies Domini:*

> If Christian individuals and families are not regularly
> drawing new life from the reading of the sacred text in a
> spirit of prayer and docility to the Church's interpretation,
> then it is difficult for the liturgical proclamation of the
> word of God alone to produce the fruit we might expect.
> This is the value of initiatives in parish communities which
> bring together during the week those who take part in the
> Eucharist—priest, ministers and faithful—in order to
> prepare the Sunday liturgy, reflecting beforehand upon
> the word of God that will be proclaimed. (#40)

Silence

Prayerful listening is fostered by an element of the liturgy of the word that is too often ignored. The lectionary calls for a period of silence after the first reading (before the responsorial psalm), after the second reading (before the gospel acclamation) and after the homily. These silences are intended to give listeners a brief time to embrace the word and to let it begin to take root in their hearts.

Liturgical ministers must become convinced of the importance of these silences. Then the assembly as a whole needs to learn how to enter into silence together and to make good use of these brief pauses. Liturgy committees need to work with lectors and musicians and presiders to make sure that ample silence is maintained as part of worship.

Because many in our society are not comfortable with silence, it is usually best to introduce a brief pause at first and then to gradually lengthen the time for reflection (perhaps up to one or two minutes). It is also important, of course, to explain the purpose of the silence and encourage all to enter into reflection together. This is a learned skill that is essential to good worship.

The Homily

The function of the homily is to break open the word of God so that it can be applied to contemporary life in the local community. The homily should usually speak to the readings of the day. However, it is also appropriate for a homily to flow from the meaning of the feast or season or from some other part of the celebration beyond the readings. Even in such cases, however, the homily still flows from the scriptures, for the Bible is the basis of our feasts and our prayer texts.

Worshipers need to see the homily as an integral part of the liturgy of the word. Just as God can speak a word to each person through the readings, God can also speak through the words of the homily. An open and attentive attitude is needed here as well as during the readings.

Much has been written about the quality of preaching in the Catholic church. The general consensus seems to be that Catholic preaching has improved greatly in recent decades, though there is clearly more room for growth. Worshipers need to understand that a homily, though spoken by one person, is always a dialogue between homilist and assembly. For the Spirit to be effective through the preacher, the hearers must be open and attentive to the same Spirit. To expect wonderful homilies every Sunday is clearly unrealistic. Preachers are gifted in different ways, and any given preacher has better weeks than others. But assemblies should expect at least an honest sharing of faith and the word of God. A truly open and seeking worshiper can usually find something of value in the homily, no matter how weak the homilist's skills.

Many Catholics hold the same misconception about the homily as about the liturgy of the word in general—that it is meant to educate. I cannot begin to count the number of times that someone has suggested to me that what I was teaching in a course or workshop should be taught to everyone through the homily on Sunday. Once again, it is important to remember that this part of the Mass seeks formation more than instruction, and that the goal is not so much learning as encounter with the living Christ. Homilists need to understand this, of course, but so do all members of the assembly.

THE CREED

The proclamation of the creed by the whole assembly is a regular part of the eucharist on Sunday and the great feasts. The Nicene Creed is not the easiest text to remember or to grasp. Often it seems

as though the assembly just rattles off the words with little awareness of or attention to what they are saying. How can we enliven our
experience of the creed so that its poetry will speak to us?

On some occasions it might work well to sing the creed, perhaps
with a refrain for the assembly while a cantor or choir sings the rest
of the text. On Easter Sunday and whenever baptism is celebrated,
we proclaim the creed in question and answer format. That provides
a fresh perspective, and perhaps it could be done occasionally at
other times as well.

Perhaps most important, the assembly needs an opportunity to
reflect on the meaning of these words. An occasional homily on the
articles of the creed could enhance the power of this ritual moment.

It can also help simply to introduce the creed with a few words
that link it to the homily or the celebration of the day. Rather than
just standing and beginning the text of the creed, during the Easter
season, for example, the presider might invite the assembly to join in
professing their faith in the God who gives us new life. Similar invi-
tations can be composed for each season or even each Sunday.

The Prayer of the Faithful

The prayer of the faithful (also called the general intercessions) has
become an expected part of our worship in the years since the Second
Vatican Council. In many parishes, however, this prayer has not yet
fulfilled its potential. The intercessions are intended to make our
prayer both current and local. This means that the petitions need to
be composed each week in the local community. Our prayers should
speak to the issues and events of the week and the needs of the local
community as well as the national and international realm.

So often this goal is missed because parishes use a published
collection of prayers. No matter how well such prayers have been

written, inevitably they are neither current nor local. They can be very useful as models for creating petitions, and local writers might draw topics or phrasing from them. The actual petitions used in any community, however, should be somewhat unique to that community and to that week in history. A generic set of petitions cannot adequately serve the purpose of the prayer of the faithful.

Members of the assembly need to understand their role in this prayer. It is called the prayer of the faithful, and it is a primary way in which the baptized fulfill their obligation to pray for others. This is why catechumens are dismissed before it is prayed. As Christ gave himself for the sake of the whole world, so his disciples are called to express their love and concern for the world in this prayer of the baptized. The prayer takes on more significance when worshipers realize that they are continuing Christ's love for the world as they pray for all those in need. The 2000 study translation of the revised *General Instruction of the Roman Missal* notes: "In the general intercessions or prayer of the faithful, the people respond in some way to the Word of God which they have welcomed in faith, and exercising the office of their baptismal priesthood, offer prayers to God for the salvation of all" (#69).

UNDER THE WORD

One of the great gifts of the Second Vatican Council to all of us today is a renewed awareness of and a wider exposure to the word of God. The liturgy of the word offers tremendous opportunities for spiritual growth. The more we help people to enter fully into this part of the Mass, the more they will grow in faith and in relationship to the living Word in our midst.

QUESTIONS FOR REFLECTION AND DISCUSSION

1. In what ways do you live your life "standing under the word"?
    Describe the role of the word of God in your own spirituality.

2. What evidence do you see that most members of your assem-
    bly understand the liturgy of the word as an opportunity to
    encounter the living Christ? Or by contrast, in what ways do
    they appear to see it as a time for education? How can we help
    people appreciate the true purpose of this part of the Mass?

3. Do the lectors in your parish proclaim the word with power?
    When this happens, does it help you to surrender to the word?

4. How would you explain the importance of listening rather than
    reading along? Do you feel the need to have the text in front of
    you while the word is proclaimed? Why or why not?

5. Do your liturgical ministers allow a significant silence after the
    first and second reading and after the homily? Does the assem-
    bly know how to enter into shared silence together? What bene-
    fits do you derive from these silences?

6. Think of instances when a homily in your parish effectively broke open the word and applied it to our own time — and instances when it did not. What makes a homily effective? What inhibits its power? How could you help your preachers improve?

7. What is your experience of the proclamation of the creed? Is it a meaningful expression of your own faith? What could make its use more effective for you?

8. Are the petitions for the prayer of the faithful composed locally each week? Are they good reflections of the needs and concerns of the community of faith? How could they be improved?

Chapter 4

Preparing for the Sacrifice

Soon after the Vatican released the new missal in 1969, an obser-
vant reporter noted that the part of the Mass following the creed
and the general intercessions was no longer called the offertory.
When he asked the papal spokesman about this, the spokesman
stressed that the change of name was deliberate because this part of
the Mass was not really the offering of the sacrifice.

More than thirty years later, however, many Catholics, including
some liturgical ministers, still call this section of the Mass by its old
name. The title given in the 1969 missal is "preparation of the gifts."

The point of the name change was to try to describe more
clearly the purpose of this portion of the liturgy. The old name suggested that this is the part of the Mass when the sacrifice is offered.
Worshipers were often encouraged to offer themselves on the paten
with the host, and this idea has lingered. In recent years, some people have even carried up a variety of items in the procession with
the gifts as symbols of offering themselves.

It is interesting to note that the name "offertory" probably derives from the Latin *ob fero,* which means to carry up front, referring to the procession with the bread and wine. This eventually was elided into *offero,* and the *offertorium* was the song that accompanied the bringing up of the gifts. Unfortunately in English the word "offertory" suggests more than a song accompanying a procession.

Calling the preparation of the gifts by the name "offertory" naturally suggests to people that they are offering something to God at that time. This is compounded by calling the collection of money "the offering."

ONE UNIQUE SACRIFICE

If one is to pinpoint a moment, the true point at which the one sacrifice is offered, it is during the eucharistic prayer. The point here is not a minor semantic issue. The letter to the Hebrews explains that in the new age begun by Christ, there is only one sacrifice acceptable to God, that of Jesus himself. The bread and wine brought to the altar are transformed into Christ when his self-offering is recalled and re-presented in the proclamation of the eucharistic prayer. We do not really offer God bread and wine or money or anything else except Jesus.

This point has important ecumenical implications. Many non-Catholic Christians have long objected to the Catholic practice of calling the Mass a sacrifice, precisely because it seemed to them that we were claiming to offer multiple sacrifices, counter to the teaching of the letter to the Hebrews.

The Mass is a sacrifice, but there is only one acceptable sacrifice made for all time, so somehow the Mass must be a participation in the one ongoing sacrifice of Christ. The eternal dimension of Christ's sacrifice is his surrender of his will to the Father's will. This was expressed clearly in the garden before his death, when he prayed that the cup might pass him by but accepted God's will rather than his own. His sacrificial decision resulted in the crucifixion and the empty tomb, but these were historical events experienced in a particular time and place. What is eternal is Christ's interior attitude of surrender to the Father, so we can say that he is forever victim and forever priest.

To share in his sacrifice requires that we submit our will to the Father's will just as Jesus did. Thus we share his sacrificial act and are caught up in him. As the second eucharistic prayer for reconciliation puts it, "Therefore, we ask you, Father, to accept us, together with your Son." Because of our baptism, we are the body of Christ and thus we can share in his sacrifice.

Pope John Paul II expresses these points clearly in his apostolic letter *Dies Domini:*

> Christ offers himself to the Father in the same act of sacrifice by which he offered himself on the Cross. "In this divine sacrifice which is accomplished in the Mass, the same Christ who offered himself once and for all in a bloody manner on the altar of the Cross is contained and is offered in an unbloody manner." To his sacrifice Christ unites the sacrifice of the Church: "In the Eucharist the sacrifice of Christ becomes also the sacrifice of the members of his Body. The lives of the faithful, their praise, sufferings, prayer and work, are united with those of Christ and with his total offering, and so acquire a new value." (#43; citations in the text are from the *Catechism of the Catholic Church,* #1366, 1368)

Sharing in Christ's sacrifice demands a lot from us, however. It means that we have to unite our wills to Christ's will. It means that we must be willing to love as he did, to suffer as he did and even to die as he did if that is necessary to remain faithful to the Father's will. This may be the most important point that many people miss about the eucharistic liturgy. If we really understood what it asked of us, we would approach each Mass in fear and trembling. We could never be casual about the meaning of this meal.

One could argue, too, that this is the core meaning of the eucharist. We are united as one body in Christ precisely because we are willing to risk our lives to imitate him. And it is because we are united as one body that we are able to join in his sacrifice to God. Thus to posit any opposition between seeing the Mass as a sacrifice or seeing it as a celebration of our unity in Christ is to posit a false problem. It is our unity that makes it possible for us to join in the sacrifice, and it is our willingness to join the sacrifice that shapes our unity.

A TIME OF PREPARATION

This part of the Mass, then, is designed for preparing the gifts for the sacrificial meal to come. The monetary gifts of the assembly are collected and brought forward along with the bread and wine. The bread and wine are placed on the altar, thus set aside for use in this holy meal. They will become the body and blood of the Lord and will then be offered to God by Christ himself.

Here is how *Music in Catholic Worship* describes the preparation of the gifts:

The eucharistic prayer is preceded by the preparation of the gifts. The purpose of the rite is to prepare bread and wine for the sacrifice. The secondary character of the rite determines the manner of the celebration. It consists very simply of bringing the gifts to the altar, possibly accompanied by song, prayers to be said by the celebrant as he prepares the gifts, and the prayer over the gifts. Of these elements the bringing of the gifts, the placing of the gifts on the altar, and the prayer over the gifts are primary. All else is secondary. (#46, in *The Liturgy Documents: A Parish Resource,* vol. 1, 3rd ed. [Chicago: Liturgy Training Publications, 1991])

While the altar and the gifts are being prepared for the eucharistic meal, all those sharing in the celebration are called to prepare themselves to enter into this sacrifice. In this sense, the preparation of the gifts is a minor part of the Mass, certainly in comparison to the eucharistic prayer and communion that follow it. This is time to prepare everything and everyone for the eucharistic sacrificial meal. This is a time for all to join themselves with Christ so that they can offer his eternal sacrifice with him.

There is perhaps only a subtle difference between this approach and the older exhortations to place ourselves on the paten as the bread is offered. The difference is between offering ourselves and preparing ourselves to unite with Christ's offering. This nuance, though subtle, is important theologically and ecumenically. I would also suggest that it may be more spiritually fruitful as well, because it focuses our attention on uniting ourselves with Christ and his submission to the Father.

Songs and Terminology

Because of our recent history of calling this part of the Mass the offertory, it is necessary to catechize the assembly about its true meaning. Yet even the best catechesis is often undone by what we actually do and say at this point in the celebration.

One of the problems is that a number of songs written for this part of the Mass since the Council have focused on offering as their theme. To choose such a song for this part of the Mass confuses the meaning of the preparation of the gifts. Fortunately, a number of songs written more recently speak clearly of preparing the altar, the bread and wine, and ourselves.

Even when a good song is chosen, however, it is sometimes announced as the "offertory song." It would be better to call it the "preparation song" or the "song during the preparation." These differences in terminology may seem small, but over time they shape the assembly's understanding of what we are doing during this part of the liturgy.

Because this part of the Mass is a minor part, it might be argued that no song is needed here. This could be a place for some silent preparation for the great eucharistic prayer that follows or for instrumental music. Worshipers might be invited verbally to use this time to prepare their hearts as the altar and the gifts are prepared.

If you choose silence over music, note that the presider is not required to pray aloud the two blessing prayers over the bread and wine. They may be spoken aloud, of course, and that may be especially appropriate on Thanksgiving Day or at other times when attention to the gifts of the field seems appropriate. But they may also be said silently by the presider, allowing the assembly to maintain their silent preparation.

Those two prayers are a bit odd here anyway. They are beautiful examples of short blessing prayers, in the style of the Jewish blessings called *berakoth*. Yet the eucharistic prayer comes from the same tradition of blessing, and it is the crucial blessing that consecrates the bread and wine. These two shorter prayers thus seem a bit redundant. It may be best to say them aloud only infrequently.

The Collection

Besides preparing themselves, the assembly also presents the bread and wine and their monetary gifts. These gestures are part of their preparation, signs of their willingness to love and serve as Jesus did. They can be a significant expression of the worshipers' commitment to follow the example of their Lord.

This powerful symbolism is often lost, however, because we have an ambivalent approach to money. Though it dominates our culture and most of our lives, we have a tendency to think of money as somehow unclean or unworthy of attention during the liturgy.

Money, of course, can easily become our false god, the god to whom we sacrifice our lives. It is precisely because this can happen, however, that we need to lift up its symbolism during the preparation of the gifts. The money we give, like the bread and wine it purchases, should be like the Jewish offering of first fruits. As the first fruits of the harvest were offered at the Temple as a symbol that the whole harvest belonged to God, so our gifts are presented as a symbol that our whole lives belong to God. We give a portion of our monetary wealth as a sign that we will use all our wealth in the service of the kingdom, according to God's will.

It is important, then, that the collection be handled reverently and prayerfully. It should certainly be part of the procession with the gifts, and it should be presented in a worthy basket or other container. Second collections should also be included in the procession, even if that means taking a few extra minutes for this part of the liturgy. (If time is a problem, consider having a second set of ministers gather the second collection just behind the first, rather than waiting until the first collection is finished to start the second.) While the first collection is usually for the needs of the parish (paying our own bills), the second collection is most often the one we really give away to those in need. This makes it a more powerful symbol of our willingness to imitate Christ in his love for the poor and the needy.

THE PROCESSION WITH THE GIFTS

One way to highlight the meaning of the assembly's gifts without adding unnecessary verbiage is simply to have those who present the gifts carry them held high over their heads. This allows all to see and suggests the importance of this symbol of the assembly's preparedness to enter into the eucharistic sacrifice. Some people may be unable to carry things this way, so exceptions can be made, but carrying the gifts so they can be seen should be encouraged.

Another challenge for pastoral practice is enlisting people to carry up the gifts. While the ushers commonly collect the monetary offerings and help arrange the procession with the gifts, other members of the assembly ought to serve as gift-bearers. This may mean scheduling families and other community members in advance, or it may work to have people volunteer for this service as they arrive at church. Sometimes ushers may need to invite people to fill this ministry if no one has been scheduled or if people do not arrive for their scheduled time. It should be a rarity that the ushers themselves present the gifts. Offer some catechesis to the assembly about the meaning of this procession. They need to know that the gift-bearers represent their brothers and sisters in presenting the gifts that symbolize the assembly's commitment and faith. They also need to see how this ritual procession is symbolic of the preparation of mind and heart to which all are called at this point in the liturgy.

It is also possible to make this procession more solemn, at least on major feasts. The participants could move more slowly, or they might be preceded by a banner, candle-bearers or a censer-bearer carrying the burning incense that will also be used to incense the bread and wine and the altar. Some communities have used liturgical dancers to lead or surround the procession. Sometimes the procession might take a different route than usual, passing through various sections of the assembly. On occasions when a fuller procession is created, the assembly might sing or the choir could offer an appropriate piece at this time.

On occasion, it might be good to use the model suggested for Holy Thursday. In this pattern, all the members of the assembly come forward in procession to present their gifts for the poor. Using this procedure occasionally on Sundays through the year might serve to remind worshipers that the collection is an integral part of their preparation to enter fully into the eucharistic prayer and communion.

From time to time the procession might begin with people bringing the altar cloth, candles and other needed items to prepare the altar just before the collection and the bread and wine are brought forward.

Just as the opening prayer is one of the oldest elements of the entrance rites, so the prayer over the gifts is one of the most ancient elements of the preparation. Once the gifts are brought forward and placed on the altar, the presider says the prayer over the gifts, indicating their purpose and pointing the assembly toward the eucharistic meal.

LEVELS OF PREPARATION

The preparation of the gifts offers the assembly an opportunity to move more deeply into the meaning of the eucharistic liturgy.

Lift up your hearts

Worshipers' preparation for the liturgy should begin at home, of course, for all that happens during the week should be the basis of our gratitude and should prompt us to give thanks in the eucharist. Preparation continues as the members of the assembly arrive for worship and join together as the body of Christ in this place. The liturgy of the word also prepares the assembly for the eucharistic meal, for Christ's words challenge us to imitate him. After the creed and general intercessions, the assembly is invited to prepare themselves even more fully as the altar and the gifts are prepared.

This brief part of the Mass called the preparation of the gifts can thus be a significant moment, a pause between the intensity of the liturgy of the word and the grandeur of the eucharistic prayer. The preparation allows time for all to align themselves more fully with Christ himself so that they can join with him in offering his sacrifice to the Father.

Questions for Reflection and Discussion

1. Have you been thinking of this part of the Mass as a preparation or as an offering? How would you explain the significance of the change of name? *Both*

2. Catholics have long called the Mass a sacrifice. How would you explain to a non-Catholic that this does not mean we are adding other sacrifices to the sacrifice of Christ?
Joining in Christ's Sacrifice

3. How can we share in the one sacrifice of Christ? How does the preparation of the gifts help you to do that?

4. Discuss the various effects of using song, instrumental music or silence during this part of the Mass. In general, which helps you to prepare more fully to enter into the eucharistic prayer? On what occasions might one be more appropriate than another?

5. How would you explain the collection as a spiritual act? How is the collection treated in your community? Is it presented as an important gift along with the bread and wine?

6. Who regularly brings up the gifts in your community? How might more members of the assembly be involved in this ministry?

7. How does your parish perform the procession with the gifts? How might it be enhanced?

8. How do most members of your assembly understand the purpose of this part of the Mass? How can we help them to use this preparation time more fruitfully?

Chapter 5

Giving Thanks and Praise

The *General Instruction of the Roman Missal,* speaking of the parts of the Mass proper to each ministry, says: "Among the parts assigned to the priest, the Eucharistic Prayer is preeminent; it is the high point of the entire celebration" (#30). The experience of many people in the assembly, however, does not quickly reinforce in their minds and hearts the centrality of the eucharistic prayer.

This is increasingly a significant issue, as the declining number of priests pushes more and more parishes to worship on occasion without a priest present and so without the eucharistic prayer. Too often we hear people speaking of communion services as if they were simply Masses with a non-ordained presider. Many Catholics do not recognize that a communion service without the eucharistic prayer is not a Mass. Their focus is almost exclusively on communion, whether it is part of a Mass or simply a communion service.

There is a danger here that we will cease to be a eucharistic community. A eucharistic community is a community that gathers to give thanks, not just a community that gathers to receive communion. Eucharist is an activity we do, not just something we receive passively. The primary activity is to thank and praise God, and we do this most explicitly in the eucharistic prayer.

Even those who recognize the theoretical importance of the eucharistic prayer sometimes find it hard to be fully invested in the prayer during the liturgy. One reason for this is that the eucharistic prayer is often seen as simply the prayer of the priest, rather than as a prayer the priest speaks in the name of the whole community. Sometimes this is a result of the way the prayer is prayed, but sometimes it flows from a false understanding that if we are not speaking the text, the prayer is not ours.

The Prayer of All

The communal nature of the prayer is suggested, at least, by the three acclamations (there are more in the eucharistic prayers for Masses with children) that are sung by the assembly as part of the prayer. Many have commented that the standard eucharistic prayers would be enhanced by adding more acclamations throughout the prayer. This would heighten the participation of the assembly and make it clearer that the prayer is intended to be prayed by all present even though only the presider speaks the bulk of the prayer. Thus far, however, the eucharistic prayers for Masses with children are the only ones that have these official additions.

The three main acclamations are linked to the three major parts of the prayer. The Holy, Holy responds to the preface, which recounts in varying ways the mighty works of God in creation and redemption. That acclamation praises God whose glory fills heaven and earth and Jesus who came in the name of the Lord. After the eucharistic prayer recalls God's wondrous deeds throughout salvation history culminating in the institution narrative, the memorial acclamation proclaims the death and resurrection of the Lord. The eucharistic prayer then adds a number of petitions and concludes with an acclamation of praise to which the assembly responds with the great amen.

A significant factor that affects how the assembly perceives this prayer is the way that it is proclaimed. If the presider truly prays the prayer in a way that invites people to join their minds and hearts with him, they will come to recognize it as a prayer that all share. If, on the other hand, the prayer is recited in a bored or monotonal fashion, it will be very difficult for the assembly to be drawn into its movement. The tone is often set by the enthusiasm (or lack thereof) with which the opening dialogue of the preface is proclaimed.

A Eucharistic People

A deeper problem, perhaps, is the lack of understanding of the nature of the eucharist itself. The very name of this sacrament, drawn from the Greek word for thanksgiving, should remind us that doing eucharist is more about giving God thanks and praise than it is about receiving communion. Communion is a result of the consecration brought about through the great prayer of thanksgiving. We gather, first and foremost, to give God thanks and praise for all that God has done for us.

Here is how Pope John Paul II puts it in his apostolic letter, *Dies Domini:*

> As the whole community gathers to celebrate "the Lord's Day," the Eucharist appears more clearly than on other days as the great "thanksgiving" in which the Spirit-filled Church turns to the Father, becoming one with Christ and speaking

in the name of all humanity. The rhythm of the week prompts us to gather up in grateful memory the events of the days which have just passed, to review them in the light of God and to thank him for his countless gifts, glorifying him "through Christ, with Christ and in Christ, in the unity of the Holy Spirit." (#42)

Worshipers need to approach the celebration with a clear awareness that they are gathering to give thanks. This can be fostered in subtle ways by the words chosen by the presider and other ministers as they speak about the gathering. More important, though, is to teach people to prepare for the eucharistic liturgy by reflecting on the preceding week to see where God has been active in their lives. This provides the basis for a sense of gratitude that leads worshipers to gather joyfully for eucharist. Of course, we always have reason to give thanks, even if it has been a terrible week, because the central reason for our thanksgiving is the death and resurrection of Christ that has won our salvation. It is helpful, however, if those gathering for worship bring with them a vivid awareness of God's blessings throughout the week. When they gather together, then, they combine their gratitude in one great prayer of thanks and praise.

Making Use of History

It might help worshipers to know just a bit of the history of the eucharistic prayer. Though the direct lines of development are not clear, one of the antecedents of the eucharistic prayer is the Jewish prayer form known as *berakah* or blessing. This prayer, which could be a simple spontaneous one or a more structured formal prayer, consists basically of a formula praising and thanking (that is, blessing) God followed by the reasons for one's gratitude and praise. The reason could be a single gift from God or, in the formal type of *berakah,* a recital of God's wondrous deeds throughout history. The formal type also added petitions that God would continue to do great things for Israel and then concluded with a doxology, a final expression of praise.

The spontaneous form of the *berakah* would be especially effective preparation for the eucharistic prayer. Orthodox Jews to this day are expected to pray dozens of such prayers each day, thanking God for everything that God gives them or does for them. This includes things we often take for granted, like another day of life, water to cleanse us, the ability to walk and work, gifts of food, or the smile of a friend. Each of these things can be a motive for thanking God throughout the day.

Such a practice, which might be adopted by Christian worshipers today, creates a constant awareness of God's gifts and a continual sense of gratitude. This would provide a solid basis for gathering together on Sunday to offer eucharist. When we wake up in the morning, for example, we might pray, "Blessed are you, Lord God, Creator of light, for you have given us another day of life." As we shower we might pray, "Blessed are you, Creator of the universe, for you have given us water to cleanse and refresh us." With every new thing we eat during the day, we could say, "Blessed are you, God who loves your people, for you give us this _ _____ to eat." Numerous times throughout each day, from the moment we awaken until we drop off to sleep again, we would be offering prayers of gratitude to the Lord. It is a prayerful way of counting our blessings. This kind of constant awareness leads to constant gratitude, and it can shape us into a truly eucharistic people.

Of course, even if many worshipers do not manage to develop a regular habit of such brief prayers of thanksgiving, simply understanding that the eucharistic prayer developed from such roots can help the assembly understand and participate more fully in the prayer.

SHARING CHRIST'S SACRIFICE

This sense of gratitude is basic to the Christian life. All that we do and are called to do as members of the church should be a response to what God has done for us. God always makes the first move. Our whole lives are a response to God's love and God's gifts.

Christ's submission of his own will to the Father's also flowed from this sense of gratitude that led him to trust in the Father's will completely. This should be the basis of our own sharing in Christ's sacrifice. Those who are deeply aware of God's love and goodness can find the courage to surrender all to God, to accept completely the Father's will. That is the way that we share in Christ's sacrificial act.

The offering of the sacrifice is focused in the eucharistic prayer, expressed in the section of the prayer immediately following the narrative of the Last Supper. In the third eucharistic prayer, for example, we pray: "Father, calling to mind the death your Son endured for our salvation, his glorious resurrection and ascension into heaven, and ready to greet him when he comes again, we offer you in thanksgiving this holy and living sacrifice." Just after we sing of Christ's death and resurrection, we are invited to share his sacrificial commitment. Preachers would do well to reflect on the significance of this commitment periodically.

THE SPIRIT OF UNITY

Liturgical formation of the assembly requires a deep awareness of the presence and action of the Holy Spirit during the eucharist. The Eastern churches have a highly developed appreciation of the Spirit's role, while in the West the Spirit has often been overlooked. Yet most of the eucharistic prayers explicitly call upon the Spirit to transform *EPICLESIS* the bread and wine and to transform the worshipers. The exception is the first eucharistic prayer, the Roman Canon, which only implies the Spirit's action; this no doubt played a role in the lack of attention to the Spirit in the West.

The first petition in each eucharistic prayer, coming generally just after the language of offering following the Last Supper narrative, asks the Spirit to grant unity to the church. This is the primary effect of the eucharist, as Thomas Aquinas made clear in the thirteenth century. Thomas taught that the ultimate purpose of the eucharist was not to transform bread and wine into the body and blood of the Lord (though it certainly does that) but to unify the church through the body and blood. Another way to say this is that the purpose of the eucharist is not just to transform bread and wine into the body and blood of Christ but to transform us into the living body of Christ.

Many Catholics still need to learn this fundamental fact about the eucharist. The communion we share with Christ brings us into communion with all the members of his body. There is no valid communion with the Lord that excludes communion with our brothers and sisters in Christ. This may become part of our sharing in Christ's sacrifice, for it is not always easy for us to accept all the members of his body. If we are to share in the sacrificial will of the one who gave himself for the whole world, however, such acceptance must be included. Sometimes the most difficult challenge worshipers face is opening up to the others with whom they worship. To be united with Christ, we must embrace his whole body.

What Is Consecrated?

Most Catholics are very aware that the bread and wine are consecrated at Mass and become the body and blood of Christ. Sometimes they link this transformation with the words of Christ at the Last Supper so closely that they miss the consecratory nature of the rest of the eucharistic prayer. The danger here is that the transformation is seen as magic, produced by saying magic formulas exactly. Rather, the consecration flows from the whole prayer proclaimed over the bread and wine, just as Christ prayed a similar prayer at the Last Supper. The narrative of that supper is part of the prayer, not an isolated magical moment that consecrates by itself.

More important is the recognition of what or who is being consecrated at the eucharist. Beyond the transformation of the bread and wine into the body and blood of the Lord, it is we who are to be consecrated in the eucharist. We are to be made holy by this sacrificial meal. We are to be shaped ever more completely into the body of Christ. We are to be consecrated again and again as his tabernacle, the primary place where he dwells in our world.

Once again this is linked to the meaning of the sacrifice. If we align our wills with the Father's will as Jesus did, we will be made holy by that very fact. If we join ourselves to Christ's sacrificial commitment, we are consecrated to his mission for the sake of the world. If we share his sacrificial act, we are offered along with him and are made holy by that offering.

Praying the Eucharistic Prayer Well

We need to offer formal catechesis and preaching about the meaning of the eucharistic prayer. Dozens of homilies could be built on the various texts found in the ten official eucharistic prayers. But the way we celebrate can also help worshipers to understand the significance of this prayer. A presider fully engaged in the prayer communicates its importance by his tone and manner.

A primary way that the liturgy indicates importance is with music. Those parts that are sung take on greater significance. If we want people to perceive the eucharistic prayer as central, it should be highlighted with music. On major feasts, this might mean singing the entire eucharistic prayer. Numerous settings of the various prayers have been published, along with the chant version found in Appendix III of the sacramentary.

If the whole prayer is not sung, perhaps the preface could be sung. If the presider is not able to sing, at least the assembly's three acclamations should be sung wholeheartedly and well. This requires using melodies that are familiar to people, as well as either a strong accompaniment or a strong song leader, or both. The three acclamations should be musically related to one another, either from the same melodic setting or at least in similar musical style. This helps the assembly to recognize the unity of the prayer as well as making participation easier.

Even when there is no accompaniment, these three acclamations should always be sung. At weekday Masses or other times when musicians are not available, the assembly can sing well-known settings of the eucharistic prayer acclamations from memory with only the presider or another member of the assembly beginning the singing to establish the pitch. If nothing else is sung at a liturgy, at least these acclamations should be sung, reminding us of the centrality of the eucharistic prayer.

Giving Thanks and Living Thanks

If we learn to live as a eucharistic people, grateful to God for all the blessings that we receive every day of our lives, we will be prepared to celebrate eucharist when we gather. Conversely, if we learn to give God thanks and praise wholeheartedly during the eucharistic liturgy, we will be more likely to notice God's gifts throughout the week. Then we will be prompted to give God thanks and praise not only with our worship but also with our lives. Thus we will fulfill the petition of Eucharistic Prayer IV: "by your Holy Spirit, gather all who share this one bread and one cup into the one body of Christ, a living sacrifice of praise."

QUESTIONS FOR REFLECTION AND DISCUSSION

1. In the past, how important was the eucharistic prayer to you? How would you explain its importance now?

2. What evidence do you see that your assembly considers the eucharistic prayer to be central? What evidence to the contrary? What could be done to heighten this awareness?

3. Do you think that your assembly recognizes this prayer as the prayer of the whole church, or just as the prayer of the presider? How could we help the assembly claim this prayer as its own? Would more acclamations help? What posture would be most conducive to that understanding?

4. Do you come to eucharist with a thankful heart? Do you think most members of your assembly do? How can we heighten awareness that the eucharist is fundamentally about praising and thanking God?

5. How might adopting the Jewish practice of prayers of thanksgiving throughout the day help you prepare for eucharist? How could such a practice be encouraged in your community?

6. Do you think that most members of your assembly recognize the unity of the community as the primary goal of eucharist? How could we help people to learn this truth of our tradition?

7. In what ways have you experienced the eucharist as consecrating and transforming you along with the bread and wine? Are you open to such transformation?

8. How do you think the proclamation of the eucharistic prayer could be enhanced in your community?

Chapter 6

Eat, Drink and Be Missionary

At the beginning of the twentieth century, many Catholics received communion only once a year. The church had been heavily influenced by Jansenism, which stressed the unworthiness of the faithful to receive their exalted Lord. Pope Saint Pius X, at the beginning of the century, urged more frequent reception of communion, and today most Catholics receive communion every time they participate in the Mass. This is surely an appropriate change in practice, because Jesus told us to take and eat, to take and drink. Sharing in communion is a culminating part of the liturgy, bringing its meaning and power to fulfillment.

However, the fact that most worshipers now receive communion regularly does not necessarily mean that they fully understand what they are doing. Even casual observation of an average parish community will reveal behavior that suggests very different understandings of what sharing in communion means. The need for more intensive catechesis in this area is apparent.

Recognizing the Body

The most obvious difference in worshipers' understanding of communion revolves around the meaning of the body of Christ. Almost all Catholics recognize the consecrated bread as the body of Christ and the consecrated wine as his blood. Some, however, seem to have missed the connection between this body of Christ in the sacramental elements (a "sacramental body") and what we call the mystical body of Christ, the community of the church.

That some people miss this connection should not surprise us; it has been a problem in the church for a long time. Saint Augustine of Hippo (late fourth to early fifth century) once chastised his church for trying to decapitate Christ. He said they thought they could have the head of the body (Christ) without the rest of the body (the church), but it is not possible to have the head without the body.

Even earlier, Saint Paul apparently encountered a similar problem among the Corinthians. In 1 Corinthians 11:29, he insists that "all who eat and drink without discerning the body, eat and drink judgment against themselves."

So the problem is not a new one, yet it is a crucial one. Too many worshipers miss both the beauty and the challenge of this mystery. The sacramental body and the mystical body are intimately intertwined. It is interesting to note, for example, that for the first half of Christian history, the term "mystical body" was applied to the sacrament, while the church itself was seen as the "real" body of Christ. In the second half of our history, that has been reversed. While one could argue for either pattern, the significant point is that these two forms of Christ's presence are so linked that they are almost interchangeable. Any understanding of the eucharist that focuses on one half of this mystery while ignoring the other half is inadequate.

Both distortions have appeared in recent years. Some people focus only on the sacramental presence of Christ and steadfastly ignore his presence in the assembly. Of course, many of us were trained in our youth to do just that—to ignore everyone around us so that they would not distract our attention from Christ. In more recent years, some people have heard church teaching about the community and have interpreted it to mean that liturgy is just a social occasion. The community that is the body of Christ is more than simply a social group. Our unity with one another and our unity with Christ are closely linked. We are branches on the one vine that is Christ; this is the source of our unity and the reason for our care for one another.

Pope John Paul II addressed the meaning of communion in his apostolic letter, *Dies Domini:*

> It is also important to be ever mindful that communion
> with Christ is deeply tied to communion with our brothers
> and sisters. The Sunday Eucharistic gathering is an
> experience of brotherhood, which the celebration should
> demonstrate clearly, while ever respecting the nature of the
> liturgical action. All this will be helped by gestures of
> welcome and by the tone of prayer, alert to the needs of all
> in the community. The sign of peace—in the Roman Rite
> significantly placed before Eucharistic communion—is a
> particularly expressive gesture which the faithful are invited
> to make as a manifestation of the People of God's acceptance
> of all that has been accomplished in the celebration and
> of the commitment to mutual love which is made in sharing
> the one bread, with the demanding words of Christ in
> mind: "If you are offering your gift at the altar, and there
> remember that your brother has something against you,

leave your gift there before the altar and go; first be recon-
ciled with your brother, and then come and offer your gift"
(Matthew 5:23–24). (#44)

RECEIVE WHAT YOU ARE

Another quotation from Saint Augustine emphasizes the link
between the sacramental body and the ecclesial body of Christ.
"Receive what you are," he preached. The old saying "You are what
you eat" takes on a new meaning in this light. Augustine reminds us
that we who receive the body of Christ are the body of Christ. By
receiving the body of Christ sacramentally, we are linked ever more
closely to the other parts of the body. Through repeated celebrations
of the eucharist, we are fashioned ever more fully into the image of
God's Son.

When the communion ministers offer the body of the Lord to
communicants, they say, "The Body of Christ." Much preaching and
catechesis can be based on those four little words. Where is the body
of Christ? His body is found in the bread, in the person in front of
you, and in all the people around you. Are you willing to swallow
the whole body of Christ? Are you willing to be the body of Christ?
This ritual formula is wondrously ambiguous because the body of
Christ is not limited to any one form of Christ's presence.

PREPARING FOR COMMUNION

The elements of the liturgy that serve as immediate preparation for
communion also can be seen as reminding us of our unity in Christ.
The first element is the Lord's Prayer, which not only speaks of our
daily bread but begins by invoking God as "our Father." God is our

Father because we are brothers and sisters of Christ and form his very body in the world today.

The second element is the sign of peace. In some liturgical traditions, the sign of peace is placed before the preparation of the gifts, in light of Christ's command to reconcile with one's brother before bringing one's gift to the altar. The Roman rite has traditionally included it as part of the communion rite. Its placement here serves to remind us clearly that communion with Christ is not opposed to communion with one another. Even more, it suggests that communion with Christ is only possible if we are willing to be in communion with one another.

The third preparatory element is the breaking of the bread and the pouring of the wine into cups for distribution, accompanied by the singing of the Lamb of God. The words that we sing in the Lamb of God remind us that Christ gave his life to take away the sins of the world. The action of breaking and pouring reminds us that Christ's body was broken and his blood was poured out for our sake. Sharing in this one bread and one cup also expresses the unity that communion fosters.

COMM-UNION

Even the word we use makes the point. Communion means "union with." It speaks of a shared union of all those who are part of Christ's body. Periodic catechesis should remind worshipers that the primary effect of the eucharist is the unity of the body of Christ. The sacramental body of Christ is intended to sustain the ecclesial body of Christ. When we receive the body and blood, we become more fully the body of Christ in the world today.

One of the ways that the liturgy itself reminds us of our unity is through the communion song. This song is intended to be sung during the communion procession, for singing unites us in one voice as we renew our unity with one another in the Lord. The song should continue throughout the distribution of communion. The revised *General Instruction of the Roman Missal* notes that the communion song is begun during the priest's reception of communion and that it "continues while the Sacrament is being ministered to the faithful" (#86). If one song is not long enough, it can be repeated or a second communion song can be added. Singing during communion should involve the whole assembly throughout the procession. After all have received, the singing ends as all enter into shared silence.

Appropriate songs for communion are those that focus on the meaning of the sharing. Songs designed for benediction or other forms of eucharistic adoration are not appropriate at communion. We do not adore Christ at communion; we share his body and blood and are thus drawn into his life.

Ending the song while much of the assembly is still in the communion procession defeats the unitive function of the song. In a similar way, different postures among the assembly during communion communicate disunity rather than unity. The revised *General Instruction of the Roman Missal* (#43) says that the people should stand from the prayer over the gifts until the end of Mass, except for kneeling at the consecration (the U.S. bishops extended this from after the Holy, Holy to after the great Amen) and sitting during the silence after communion. This implies that all who are able would be standing during the whole communion procession. Once everyone has received, then all sit for silent prayer together. This also means, of course, that the assembly remains standing during the dialogue just before communion ("This is the Lamb of God who takes away . . . ") rather than kneeling as is the custom in many parishes.

Efforts to change customs toward a common posture and congregational singing that lasts throughout the communion procession will help the assembly to sense the unity of this action. Regular catechesis is necessary, but parish practice must be in accord with the catechesis to promote deeper understanding.

Both Species

Sometimes it is helpful to consider our pastoral practice from the viewpoint of a stranger in our midst. How odd it must seem to such a visitor when in many parishes a significant number of people do not follow Christ's dual command at the Last Supper to eat his body and drink his blood! Even though we repeat Christ's words in every Mass, many people seem to ignore the second command of the Lord. We continue to believe that Christ is wholly present under either form of bread or wine, but it is clear that the full symbolism of the sacrament requires both elements. Christ gave us both his body and his blood to emphasize the completeness of his self-giving and his enduring presence with us. The Second Vatican Council restored the sharing of Christ's blood, and many Catholics have embraced this manner of receiving communion in the years since the Council. Yet many others seldom, if ever, share the blood of the Lord.

Of course, in some parishes the fault lies with a pastor or liturgy committee that does not offer both species at all Masses. But even when the cup is offered, many people do not partake. While some people avoid the cup because of hypersensitivity about germs, many simply do not understand the meaning of the cup. They need to hear about the Old Testament blood of the covenant as a sign of unity between God and the people. They need to think about Christ's blood, poured out for them. They need to follow the martyrs of Revelation who washed their robes in the blood of the Lamb.

They need to recognize why Christ used both food and drink to communicate his bodily presence. Every time I preach on the meaning of communion under both species, people tell me after Mass that they have never heard these things before. They should be part of the continuing liturgical catechesis in every parish.

SILENCE

After all have received communion, there is an opportunity for the assembly to sit together in shared silence for reflection and prayer. Many people feel the need for such silence and try to enter into it during the communion procession. The proper time for this, however, is after all have received and are seated. If silence is not provided at this time, of course, we should not be surprised that some people will ignore the communion song in order to seek some time for prayer and reflection.

This should be a time for silence, not a time for choral or solo music that feels like a performance. Though instrumental music might be acceptable, there is also value in learning to keep prayerful silence together. Many people have little or no silence in their daily lives; keeping silence together at liturgy can be a school for learning to seek silence regularly.

The *General Instruction of the Roman Missal* speaks of the assembly spending some time in silence after the communion procession and then adds that "either a psalm or other canticle of praise or a hymn may be sung by the entire congregation" (#88). This does not mean a choral or solo offering, but a song sung by the whole assembly. This song of praise could occur after a time of silence. It might replace the recessional hymn, so that the Mass actually ends with the words "The Mass is ended; go in peace."

Dismissal to Mission

Once the prayer after communion concludes the communion rite, the liturgy moves into a brief dismissal rite. It begins with any announcements that need to be made to the parish community. Announcements are placed here because they offer ways that the community can carry out in the coming week the commitments they have made during the liturgy. They are to go forth to live as the body of Christ all week. This can be more obvious if the announcements indicate the linkage. For example, "As we have shared at the table of the Lord, all are invited to help serve food at the soup kitchen next Saturday." Announcements should be few and should concern the whole community or something that is happening right after Mass. Other information should be communicated through the parish bulletin or newsletter.

After the announcements, the liturgy concludes with a blessing and a formula of dismissal. Use of the solemn blessings or the prayers over the people can be helpful in suggesting links between the liturgy and the daily lives of the worshipers.

The dismissal formula is brief but it can also be a fertile basis for preaching and catechesis. Unfortunately, our English translation of this formula does not make clear the fullness of its meaning. The Latin *Ite, missa est* could be literally translated as "Go, it is the *missa*"; that is, "Go, it is the sending" or "Go, you are sent."

Being sent means being assigned to carry on the mission of the church. Those who are sent are apostles (a title that means those sent). The dismissal from the liturgy is not just an ending but also a beginning. What we have celebrated together, we are sent forth to live out during the week.

Here is how Pope John Paul spoke of the connection between Mass and mission in his apostolic letter, *Dies Domini:*

> Like the first witnesses of the Resurrection, Christians who gather each Sunday to experience and proclaim the presence of the Risen Lord are called to evangelize and bear witness in their daily lives. Given this, the Prayer after Communion and the Concluding Rite—the Final Blessing and the Dismissal—need to be better valued and appreciated, so that all who have shared in the Eucharist may come to a deeper sense of the responsibility which is entrusted to them. Once the assembly disperses, Christ's disciples return to their everyday surroundings with the commitment to make their whole life a gift, a spiritual sacrifice pleasing to God (cf. Romans 12:1). (#45)

This relationship between our worship and our daily lives is perhaps the theme that needs the most preaching and catechesis. Our secular culture inclines us to separate religion and the rest of our lives. It takes constant effort to remember that all of life belongs to God and all that we do in worship is meant to shape the rest of our lives. Then, in turn, we bring back to worship all that happens during the week, especially our gratitude for all that God has done for us. Thus liturgy and daily life support and shape each other.

Continuing Formation

When we began the reform of the liturgy after the Second Vatican Council, the need for catechesis was obvious. Though we were handicapped by a scarcity of liturgically educated clergy and catechists, most parishes made some attempt to communicate to parishioners the reason for the changes and some sense of liturgical history and theology. However, those efforts were several decades ago and many members of the church today were not even alive at that time. They need liturgical formation, too.

Liturgical education and formation are needed continually in every parish. People need to know something of the history of our liturgical tradition. They need to know their proper role during the liturgy. They need, above all, guidance in learning how to enter into the meaning of the liturgy so that it can shape their lives and form them into the image of Christ their Lord. Then the hopes of the Second Vatican Council may begin to be fulfilled, as a renewed people of God carries on the mission of Christ to renew the world.

Questions for Reflection and Discussion

1. In your community, how strongly felt is the link between the sacramental body of Christ and the mystical body?

2. When you receive communion, are you conscious of "receiving what you are"? How often do you think of yourself as part of the body of Christ? What effect does this have on you?

3. In what ways do the Lord's Prayer, the sign of peace and the breaking of the bread help you to remember your unity with your brothers and sisters in Christ?

4. What posture does your assembly take during the communion procession? Do you see the importance of a common posture?

5. Is the communion song in your community appropriate and sung well? Does it last for the full length of the communion procession? What would help the assembly enter more fully into this song and to experience in their unity in Christ?

6. Is communion offered under both species at all Masses in your community? If not, why not? What might help people to understand more fully the reasons for receiving both?

7. Does your community enter into a significant shared silence after all have received communion?

8. When you are dismissed from the eucharistic liturgy, do you feel sent out on mission? What could help people make the connections between their worship and living the gospel all week?